Conversation with Murasaki

Also by Tom Lowenstein:

The Death of Mrs Owl
Eskimo Poems from Canada and Greenland
Filibustering in Samsara
Filibustering in Samsara — A Footnote
The Things That Were Said of Them
Ancient Land: Sacred Whale
Sea Ice Subsistence at Point Hope, Alaska
The Vision of the Buddha
A Social History of Tikigaq, Alaska
Ancestors and Species: New and Selected Ethnographic Poetry
Classic Haiku
Ultimate Americans: Point Hope, Alaska: 1826–1909

Tom Lowenstein

Conversation
with
Murasaki

Shearsman Books
Exeter

First published in the United Kingdom 2009 by
Shearsman Books Ltd
58 Velwell Road
Exeter EX4 4LD

ISBN 978-1-84861-065-1
First Edition

Acknowledgements
Sequences in this volume were published as follows:

'Pre-dynastic Essays' in *Poetry Review*
'Existence Mazurkas' in *PN Review*
'An Hour and a Half with Hiroshige' in *The New Cambridge Review*
'Secondary Presences' in *Signals* (online)
'Dragonfly Intelligence' in *Tears in the Fence*
'Conversation with Murasaki' in *London Review of Books*
'Hototogisu – Japanese Cuckoo' in *Fulcrum* (New York)
'Notebook Hokku', 'Everywhere Wrong Bodies'
'Starting as a Ruin' (in earlier sequence) in *Poetry Review* and *Shearsman* magazine
'Sehnsucht Nectar' in *Poetry Salzburg Review*
'The Poverty of Pots and Jars' in *Great Works* (online)
a selection from 'No Pond Moment' on www.londongrip.com

Many thanks to all editors concerned.

Cover art: Toyokuni III 'Prince Genji in a Court Room', 1852.
Photograph by Jemimah Kuhfeld.

Contents

For Anna

I

An Hour and Half with Hiroshige

1.

I know what you mean by this hypertrophically engorged blossom.
It's in storybook snow-clots, which bounce, on the one hand,

(ping pong) off the eyeball and proclaim ways, on the other,
in which emphasis implies concealment or (implied) withholding,

and that what appears, at first glimpse, on the surface,
to be gross, supplies situations of seclusion for the essences

which otherwise could never be arrested
or, at the least, expressed and apprehended.

2.

They can't be kept from one another's clutches,
this orang-utan orange and barefaced green screeching.

A pine that's endured transects and referees their unappetising wrangle.
Spring's juices run bitter. Autumn's shame is raw and spiteful.

3.

Ah, plums! how greedily you'll plump out fructified, in full, from these
       rude,
forced, crude, harsh unaccommodated clusters, suspended, all too soon
       and often
in fly-punctuated, mildew-sprinkled and wasp-punctured pruinescence.

4.

I used to grow that iris. But decorum forbids
the disclosure of what habit-formingly it once dictated.

Still, it's glandular already, and with heartening
apartness—autochthonously valiant—stands.

5.

(It's not the same with maple,
which keeps strictly to species,

and for this glaring interval
contrives, rudely, to blind us.)

6.

What is this waste of a good, high, full moon, fissiparously
obscured by chains of wild geese on their equinoctial voyage?

Let all of them have flocked south from the Kuril Islands, and when
they've settled, you can re-install this expatriated item to its intact hangar.

7.

The sea was a dragon, and – in its adolescent phase of
mustard kale whose fretwork was etched or splash-frozen
on the mountain – there was, all at once, arrest and impulse.

Froth granules have evolved to rock. But whether
this stone-and-water cobalt will eventually dissolve,
is the inhabiting enigma of this least chemical of deposits.

8.

No good gaping at volcanos yet. Better first
to clear the intervening landscape of all these
fussy and obfuscating by-products of custom.

9.

Too much ostentatious blue makes us
tend to forget that our day-trip to those
maples was construed as pilgrimage originally.

We set out *qua* sophisticated aestheticians
and hyper-refined, dissatisfied literati.
And see how seducingly we've been so far sated!

10.

What a burden it became to carry on
as modern. For we never could displace
ourselves from these shrunk ends

of the present, and thus, unfathomably,
fell foul of lotuses we'd blundered into.
How gorgeous, nonetheless, they kept on growing!

11.

A single full moon reflected
in ten thousand fields of paddy.

Why repine at this equalising
circulation of an institution?

12.

No, no, no. Not these transitory people.
Just water in movement and some experienced
old pine branches. Don't reflect me there either.

13.

Trees lined the beach and, hypothetically,
you strolled between them. People had this

experience *circa* 1740 (that leisure took effort),
then projected it, perfected, as a recollection.

14.

High across the gulch through autumn,
strenuous, the bridge continues.

It is the joining power of your walk.
And all, thus extended, conspires towards outcome.

15.

A low intensity containment within this slopingly
inflected frame's shallow, unemphatic bevel.

No need to go deep. It's much better on the edge,
from where you can glance at whatever travels near you.

No Pond Moment

> Ancient pond.
> A frog jumps in.
> The sound of water.

> Matsuo Basho

1.

Slicing though its own
reflection the frog silently
embraced its disappearance.

2.

In the stone of the rim, there was
jumping and splashing.
But nothing could rattle the water surface.

3.

I'd like to believe the frog was
just pursuing its genetic *dharma*.
How you are to everyone—is all they'll notice.

4.

Deep in the mountains,
unwitnessed millions

of leptodactylids
reiterate the moment.

5.

Born 1643 and died at just fifty.
A transient specimen of plantain
that underwent exposure.

6.

As he stooped to undo them,
damp blue lashings
revealed gently webbed sandals.

7.

Frog spawn: and a bulge of
pop-eyed Bodhidharma faces
glaring from behind a lotus.

8.

(Humourless as carp
that mopped up the tadpoles
inseminating this pond water.)

9.

Jump at just the right angle
and you might cancel your reflection.
Was this frog cognition?

10.

The frog cogitated and took off.
Nothing was the same and not much
changed in a gently wetted cosmos.

11.

Abandoning land and achieving deep water,
the frog had arrived in a boundaryless vicinity.
No sacred places left to visit.

12.

In the water of his mind, no pond
to jump in. The poet said this.
The frog knew no better.

13.

A good small place
for a diagram of time
before it stopped working.

14.

He too took a voyage through the labyrinth of history.
Solitary, transmogrified but still identical to all the others.
Even the Buddhas have maintained their practice.

15.

Slumbering universal water. The frog swam
to the bottom where the world's umbilical

coiled upward from its root mud to a lotus.
There were plenty of mosquitoes and he ate a number.

16.

First here and now gone. It adopted
a familiar but unfathomable medium.
The word *gone*'s implication.

17.

The frog that spawned successive
energetic generations. Which individuals
have been witnessed jumping?

18.

Everything has
a career
of some description.

19.

A remote stretch of water.
Ten thousand frog throats
lifted to extol the silence.

20.

Hard to quantify the moment when that
ounce-and-a-half landed. Followed by
three centuries of measured syllabic splashing.

21.

Afternoon garden. Downward entry.
Below the surface, one solitary venture converged
with the All in an inaccessible resolution.

22.

A hole in the water that led
twistingly to the underworld.
This small messenger connected us.

23.

'Why not sit quietly?' 'Because something makes
me want to jump, if just once. Isn't it natural
to fribble away your energy and talent?'

25.

Evolving towards the space,
unprompted,
that the man left empty.

26.

is an endnote,
here omitted.

27.

From facts on land to beyond
in the water. What's unsaid is
what no longer happens.

28.

This garden with its patterned stones
and variegated maple and saxifrage
plantings is too painfully beautiful.

I must therefore leave it.
The uniformity of water calls me.

29.

The time has arrived for a short pause
in this turmoil.
Something dived in at a deeper angle.

30.

A minor alarum. Eructation of the water.
Of how many tones
was the key note compounded?

(Raise them inchingly by vibe
and they'll scratch some planet.
A mechanical jangle that may reach us some evening.)

31.

One thing has become another.
In time they will belong together.

The frog slipped off as quietly as it could.
Mindful of Zen etiquette *et cetera*.

32.

The red metal edges of the maple. Buds
in late winter transmit soft green noises.
Curious small ones. Generating observation.

33.

I would like to have said 'as though'.
But it was veritably so.

Lips of the water non-appropriatively
swallowing. This we lived near to.

34.

A small cold noise in a blue white
green and grey tonality. A smooth
stone: low. Impermanent as an eternity.

35.

Spiral. Everything evolves in
its endogenous reflexive coil.

So too, this insignificant interpolation.
Was there majesty in anything?

36.

By the mythologically terrific rock fall,
issued these infernal hissings
of the creative primal serpent.

But what I heard was nothing heroic.
I listen to it twice daily just under
the surface of my soup bowl's contents.

37.

The floating leaf's resistance
as the frog clambered to its surface.
Were there more in the offing?

38.

It's change finally that happened.
The light wind on its body
traced an epic passage.

39.

Brain flash, mediated by the lotus stem
that feeds in the muck and wanders
to the surface, detonates its flowering.

Launched in the water the frog had no trouble
reconnoitring the silence.
Every midday tension sublimates eventually.

40.

Was that a frog? Or was it Avalokiteshvara as he coursed
the three worlds and identified the emptiness of all self-being?
Before that, even, every Buddha was a monkey.

41.

The weather was mixed.
The banana tree ached
to be somewhere else in Asia.

The frog in Japan was happy with its station.
All things evolve along
personal conduits of transmigration.

42.

In spring rain and wind, no stable reflections.
Cherry blossom, bobbing over ruffled
water, getting yellow at the edges.

43.

Neither frog nor water, but the sound
of the one as it entered the other.
Momentary and, in some ways, lasting.

44.

It was no particular individual
generated the long-hand that by reflex
issued from the trajectory of its impulse.

Thereafter in *hiragana*, three modest
and quick drying ink inscriptions
on a page that might well have

received anything. All objects
quintessentially anonymous.
Your name, likewise, a miscalculation.

45.

Autumn. It's been raining.
Lotus pads in tatters. Nowhere
to sit now. One final effort.

46.

Reports of these moments. Their importance
has become the import. Reputation.
Publication. And a history of such matters.

47.

Unbroken surface and the splash of water
synonymous in time gone.
A few inches of calligraphy.

48.

Meaningful-seeming stone.
And some particle
inside it still in motion.

A volcano exploded.
A long croak of rubble
there was no-one to hear then.

49.

Point A and the next one from a
third location. Things detected in
their separation join up for a moment.

50.

Spontaneity at centre.
It was audience that mattered.
Subject and object a one-way transaction.

51.

Nescient of *dukkha*. *I*'s pain
tangled in the hair roots.
Momentary interruption.

52.

A squamous individuality had effectively gone forward.
This was an occasion to detach from custom.
Still, skin to surface tension, here on, its reflection glittered.

53.

First Basho jumped. Next Ryokan.
Then Sengai followed.
Names in the water washed off with the splashes.

54.

Trickster sat by the pond's edge. He was hungry,
as ever. He took out his *usuk* to send it hunting.

'My, I'm hungry!' Trickster went on saying.
Night fell. He had lost his *usuk*. That's what happened.

55.

It was beautiful, this stage, on
which everything was a painting.

The time came then when it drifted away
beyond the solution of a representation.

Towards a realm of the opposite
it took that single step—and then
deep into freedom's unlimited vicissitudes.

56.

It's form and nothing
that
the mind jumps into.

57.

No, there was
n't
a silence

Conversation with Murasaki

1.

Murasaki—I imagined
a dye the colour of mulberries.
A burnet moth's underwing.

2.

She brushes past Sei Shonagon.
Sleeves in tension.
Both brushes charged with silken resistance.

3.

When she sang it was brocade.
When she modestly whispered,
a most delicate embroidery.

4.

'Her sash matched her robe.
But did you notice the lining of her sleeve?
I could have laughed all evening!'

5.

The wisteria in its tub, whose ancient stem
and transient clusters you comprehended clearly,
but which you did not know how to prune.

6.

How many such cultivated
and also promiscuous ladies
have I wished to have been acquainted with?

7.

Late afternoon rain,
then sun on the raspberries—
I so wanted to show you.

8.

How vulgar would you think it
to express my predilection
for these extra yellow quinces?

9.

Please tell me: how, culturally, could we
be more different? Yet I, with minor, bemused
reservations, am drawn entirely to your aesthetic.

10.

So many little rules.
How delicious to break one!
We'll mend these fragments into something.

11.

His long night's escapade.
Does inherited custom demand
rupture of tradition?

12.

Dilapidated mansion. Tangled thickets.
Behind a screen,
she waits for moon-rise.

13.

Having sunk to this obscurity
she still plies the koto.
No one behind screens to listen.

14.

Shut in from sunlight,
she keeps company with rain and music.
Wasting beneath powder.

15.

What happens in the *Genji*?
Births, fixation, death and an eroticism by subterfuge
delayed tantalisingly by the complicated exchange of waka.

16.

The plum which in the 16th century was
supplanted by the cherry. Aesthetically staggered,
do they now blossom in competition?

17.

Lamp light. Moon-rise.
I look up.
Does the moon, too, say 'I'?

18.

The floating world.
We move within it.
It. We. Tangle and illusion.

19.

High above the city, he searches out
two things that grow together:
wild herbs and the sutras.

20.

It is comparatively simple to satisfy desire.
But to die without studying the sutras . . .
Still, it makes little difference.

21.

A poignant meditation on the doctrine of *anicca*.
Then all at once
they're playing football.

22.

Guarding against presenting things
only in the best possible taste,
thus he expressed an asymmetrical aesthetic.

23.

A trunk that grew lichen.
A stone that happened to
lie on the mountain.

24.

I know how loud and irregular noises
disturbed you. I too live
in your ideal silence.

25.

To be old and still young.
At once female and male.
We are all one person.

26.

You would be astonished
At the squalor of European history.
But you would have liked Jane Austen.

27.

Spirit possession.
The hysterical luxury
of existence as two people.

28.

No longer even dust.
Your *you* became
someone else's brush strokes.

29.

Waley on his deathbed.
Neither he nor his space.
But now equal with not-you in north London traffic.

30.

'Genji was dead. And there was no one like him.'
Punks eat sushi.
Mono no aware. Lacrimae rerum.

31.

These msn and My Space girls whose virtual selves
fire off keyboard fantasias: they, as with Genji's
women, gossip apprehensively behind their screens.

32.

There they all must be in
Ambitabha's garden, where birds
and rivers sing unintelligibly in Sanskrit.

33.

The Bridge of Dreams joins two empty spaces.
We hurried from one near end's surface
oblivious of where we may have started.

34.

Hokku faxed from a tobacconist.
Syllabically hopping,
to Tokyo they yo yo.

Hototogisu — Japanese Cuckoo

1.

From the realm of the dead it
exits each spring with blood in
its singing—*hototogisu.*

2.

What, underworld migrant, will
your message next year tell us?
The world's darkness is sufficient.

3.

Blood-coughing song bird:
consent to the nightingale's effort
to harmonize the emblem.

4.

Throat-blood.
Rice growth.
Hades cuckoo.

5.

Stammer in a liquid pattern,
hototogisu, up to the light
where lovers gladden.

6.

Scroll full of cuckoos.
Quick to accumulate.
Hard to sing with.

7.

All night I hear
the cat and the vixen.
Bat-wing wrinkles.

8.

Where was I dreaming—
flat stone—
in the underworld?

9.

From Hades vale, where a fox
prince had engaged her: haunted,
repeated *hototogisu* tooting.

10.

Late Schubert 4th movement.
Death and a cuckoo
in the thicket.

11.

Do throat blood and bird song come
from one same thoughtful inclination?
Hototogisu's disequilibrium.

12.

Reborn, restless, gone wrong,
and repeating, little
cuckoo of samsara.

13.

Long, long dead and longing to relive
my days with loved ones trapped
in longing for the dead who've left them.

14.

Spondee and anapaest
plaintively completing
hototogisu's lumina nocte.

15.

That song announcing spring
arrived with heart's blood. But
all I could hear was cuckoo burble.

16.

With dragon's blood still enlivening
his palate, the hero withdrew
from the cuckoo's messuage.

17.

Solemn old willow.
The *hototogisu* pursues
its solipsistic isness.

18.

As men cudgel their wits,
so the cuckoo
eludes them.

19.

Cool beneath the willow. But it's
not as we thought. *Hototogisu*
far off sings its admonition.

20.

Cuckoo tantrum.
Auspices and bird shout.
Ava-tili-guuvaq.

21.

Bless that cuckoo, poet, when
it flies in from the dead and
drops hell's faeces on you.

22.

Ambivalent egg of the *hototogisu*—
we'll incubate it in this
empty stanza.

23.

Poets who went mad
in contemplation
of the cuckoo's potential.

24.

Experts who spout
which has given the cuckoo
a traumatizing asthma.

25.

What the Sibyl transcribed in her
grotto at Cumae had been adumbrated
by her psychopomp the *hototogisu.*

26.

Overwhelmed by expectation,
the cuckoo was asphyxiated by
spring breezes it brought with it.

II

Existence Mazurkas

1.

A long expensive journey. The landscape
grown stranger. A space at the end
where there's no more to interpret.

2.

Neither one, three nor seven.
An existence, merely, of the four initial
bars of crochet rests or in Alberti figuration.

3.

Everything's about the one,
the three, the four and seven,
returned from their epic.

4.

When everyone had seen
the three, an old horse was
turned out into the meadow.

5.

A line that ran on that was lost
for breath. The *son filé* left nothing
but a round extant exuberance of quiet.

6.

A line whose rhythm from this
core of pine had shaped its heart with
such comparatively indecisive graphite.

7.

Why couldn't he have taken that one extra step towards
those blowsy and dishevelled gladioli?
The grave extolled downward. Genitals an extinct reptile.

8.

One headstone was eaten
and another
had burst in desiccated exudation:

laid a century before the grape
hyacinths and bluebells shook
their heads through its unifying shadow.

9.

To be passers-by in history was
all they ever claimed. And history
itself was a temporary visitor.

10.

Dead now and another. Corrupted
as the dog's testicle orchid which haplessly
deliquesces at the archivist's window.

11.

Sitting with the cat and reconnected with my person,
it was hard to remember that I'd ever been away
and had failed to apply for permission to re-enter.

12.

The old cat buzzes out the same old tune.
'I have no self. I do not love. There is no
death. Excepting digestion and defecation.'

13.

A melange of anthropological
topics subsumed in a
paragraph or two of Virgil.

These converged in the river
that came drumming on
our bodies as we hesitantly piloted.

14.

This horrifyingly divagated meander
in which the stream is denied by
its source and turned back by the ocean.

15.

Displacement existence. Time's
parallel avowal and its
progress through the forest.

16.

At Basho's 'changing and unchanging',
two swans fly through a panel
of dark, scarce sunlight.

17.

Continuum of non-existence
interrupted by this interesting
temporary interlude.

Dragonfly Intelligence

1.

Hunting at twilight
low on the river
a solitary dragonfly.

2.

Freaked beneath the willow
in fringes of current and lily stem
reflections, a grooved fan advances.

(Nothing on marsh marigold
leaves but some species, gone now,
that took off there).

3.

Wings stained indigo in patches
across slow, dark water.
Gun-metal-male pursues

green armoured filigree for on-the-
wing congress in Vatsyayana's
'splitting-the-bamboo' and 'clasping' postures.

4.

Stagnant water. But through open
patches in the muddled dross of
weed rot, she presses her enamel.

5.

A kestrel transects a line across the marshes.
Between the pylons, a dragonfly hunting.
For every life, the circumscription of its trigonometry.

6.

Eye facets shuffle. Wings angle
downward. By the weeds in the
ditch, it basks on asphalt.

7.

Unidentifiable *aeshnid* holding
its position in a chimney of
mosquitoes. Mild wind at twilight.

8.

I don't have to know your species
any more than you cognize
my presence: but guess if you

show one stripe more on the thorax
than the *Enalagma*, you have this
or that identity. Which both matters and doesn't.

9.

Some old Swedish minister one evening
alighting on taxonomy
that so fitted this insect.

10.

What I never could touch
were those transpositions,
swifter and more supple than

the movement up of sub-
aquatic plant growth, where
the nymph in its armour

threads a passage and by jet
propulsion feeds towards
its ariel, climactic pruinescence.

11.

Lucifer, pupating in the ooze
who never saw light until through slits
in the chitin of his body armour

pumped ichor out through wing
reticulations and thereby reconnected
with the star he was born in.

12.

Experience and combine. What felt hard
underfoot was swept by the same wind
as these dragonflies that cruise against it.

13.

Along the slats of the table in
the garden by the reservoir the
tree has dropped some long stems

where last night I picked these
small sour cherries. And now at
midday, asymmetrically, three

damselflies have settled, and their
sharp blue abdomens—as though titrated
from a noon sky between cloud-breaks

in the water and alongside the slender
curve of cherry stems, still green as
they're drying—are disposed in patterns.

14.

Indomitable *quadrimaculata* that blackened
the sky over Malmö in 1890: how is it
I find you, dried mechanically by ants

that have tunnelled from your eyes and
down through the abdomen, wings spread
stiff in permanently grounded aspiration?

15.

Basking in October sun, the red
Sympetrium, brown wings flexed and
fossilised anachronistically on tarmac.

16.

Small exquisite things:
the dragonfly's line of
inextinguishable poetry.

17.

In apple green and sky blue segments,
the lavender is complemented by a stalk,
suspended vertically, that settles on it for a moment.

18.

Damselflies of Japan: how often did
you leave those green reeds bowing
merely to late wind and shadow?

Your impeccable morning of a brittle,
tightly-flexed kimono sinks to twilight
in Hokkaido as the summer on our necks

discloses the perfection of your finish
and all we had surmised of our own
far-fetched and comprehensive incompleteness.

19.

Zygopterids' pretense, in masquerade,
competing for position in the order amid
seniors that bite harder and more deeply.

20.

One final dragonfly coasting in November
sunlight. No hope. No fear of death.
Simply knows to keep feeding.

The Poverty of Pots and Jars

1.

All beginning in a pot
outlasted, to the urn's last,
this generous container.

2.

Potential, repletion, liberality, storage.
The interior intangible, the skin utilitarian.
What the maker abandoned became her donation.

3.

Exuberant and shy, both.
The inside and the surface
mutually alluding.

4.

Aged with fifteen years of pickle, so dense
now that inter-spicing has transformed
the jar wall to a rind—transitionally edible.

5.

It's a rind minus fruit. A form quintessentially
that's without. And for all our beautiful discarded
peel, it's our frangible, tangible compensation.

6.

Together we embrace the convex.
But thorough the inside:
that's a solitary expedition.[1]

7.

O the mildness. Still thing. Earth's courtesy
that's transcended between hands. No angular
fragments with their inconclusive edges.

8.

Here, through history,
was a blameless tool.
One simplifying utensil.

9.

A renewed fragmentation.
Crazed alignment which had,
just once, shuddered.

---

[1] thorough—both with today's and the 17th century's meaning of 'through'.

10.

The pot that renounced its continuity.
Milk which meant well. That
opening face. O darling of a horizon!

11.

Through glass manufactured
to the transparency of self-abnegation,

a gathering of perfectly contrived minor enclosures
whose shared darkness was both local and Korean.

12.

Pale green nude lotus
whose inscription on biscuit
healed scorching bodies.[2]

13.

The nature of the various,
subordinated to a state of
of one simply jarred thing.

14.

At once one-year-old and mother.
Innocence from centre
which both thrusts and renounces.

---

[2] biscuit — fired but unglazed pottery

15.

Unmemorable interior. Mortality
in the concave. A flicker
of the conscious in *free* time.

16.

Let me retreat to this unvarnished
corner where the jars stand helpless,

each with its shadow which crawls up
and then falls as the window determines.

17.

No more about pots. The world's a full
enough container and spins without a
pedal on its motionless, self-generating secret.

Pre-dynastic Essays

1.

Family of red-grey finger-spotted brush-dabbed
scenes of crocodile and ibis. Dead now, they're laid
flat. They'll swim no longer or go feed in the shallows.

2.

Blue hands that grasped.
A lump from the river and its
bone-dimensioned fruition.

3.

Anonymous the makers who let
go of this vessel, balancing
their time with function.

4.

Curio and revenant passed from
daylight to become a number.

These were infinite things that
were animated by a few coins.

Everything was made a god.
And so re-created one another.

5.

A bead and an inscription.
Auspicious donations.

Adjusted to shadow,
(some finger dropped them)
enacting chthonic negotiations.

6.

The object never was
to displace the light
but to contain darkness.

7.

Black waves over glaze.
That these had meaning
was her cemetery meditation.

8.

A quiet where they'd jar
his ashes: bone-meal
rapping the bark of an apple.

9.

Surface dictates thing not person.
What was human translated
to an artefact that's wanted.

10.

The status of the container and
the expedition of its outflow.

These became reconciled
to an alternating concurrence.

11.

The smaller it looked, the more singularly
it created light. Shut, so I thought, to
its seed idea without verbal affirmation.

12.

Plain pots that stopped
at the point of their use.
And thus they healed us.

13.

Selves in transition. The onlooker
who became a relic with its
consequent accession number.

14.

Photo from the nineteen twenties
encapsulating four millennia
of summers in a computer revival.

15.

Earth that's fetched up in this cabinet
demands
no admiration we naively offered.

16.

Contained or interred.
In absolute darkness
were no dilemmas.

17.

Soul-house with seats by the
terracotta window. So to watch
the dead return from river-bathing.

18.

Ritual that generated domestic utensils.
Subsistence stuff apportioned within
this unadulterated circumference.

20.

As breath to water:
so
these amplitudes.

Postscript on Making

1.

As it spins through the fingers, she breathes
this poor thing through a first transition.
Its centre empty and for ever in question.

2.

Numen, as the walls build from
the pedal, the clay, before she started,
held this emptiness movement.

3.

Were you there when I pierced these with a bird-
bone needle and threaded them with sinew?
Slight, at the pot's base, dust of that connective.

4.

A convex that ached. But no
procreation. Another had feeling.
And our soft gaze was reflected.

5.

The mud of old Nile where ibis on their
angled legs had waded. Cross-hatched,
crocodiles dragged sullenly along it.

6.

Terracotta fragment fallen to
this rehabilitated cranium
where a thought once flickered.

Notebook Hokku

1.

Low grey cloud. Against
the wind, the melancholy weight
of one last heron.

2.

Invisible across the field
the echo of an axe
among the cricket willows.

3.

Cold summer wind. And
unripe apples, tossed up, thump
the light green under foliage.

4.

Immobile and clotted, black
fly submit to red ants' traffic
on the runner bean stalk.

5.

Inside the ruins of this fallen
willow: damp earth, fungus
and dry white fruit stones.

6.

As the flycatcher
pirouettes,
the globe revolves with it.

7.

Silence huge. A solitude without limit.
What moves through these spaces?
Not I but a function.

8.

Picking through a bowl of damsons.
Fame, success, enlightenment.
These are well-construed notions.

9.

Damsons in handfuls echo
in the basin. Quiet between
mouth and a dark blue flavour.

10.

Bird song was scrolled
tightly, as I walked beside
the elder, between umbels.

III

Secondary Presences

1.

It is the world composes.
A writer
its amanuensis merely.

2.

Nothing to pencil beyond
some ritualised behaviour on
this anthropocene prairie.

3.

Pencil re-engages with the surface
it researches. An archaic conversation.
As cranes' feet trampled the Euphrates delta.

4.

Which is it matters: these problematic
assonantal choices or the trees themselves
dictating their syllabic instigation?

5.

(But then how do the two eventually
converge on this triangle of graphite
that presses the hand forward?)

6.

No enchantment in the
syllable beyond what it
acquires by interrelation.

7.

Every syllable a risk; a trespass.
Crude integument of pencil that briefly
surrounds that tentative initial embryo.

8.

Movement forward from this 14th century apple.
Grafted by Chaucer. Shakespeare ate it.

Browne and Marvell contemplated and enclosed it.
Milton incubated and then hatched the maggot.

9.

(Keats identified
the apple and
divined its centre.)

10.

Flies take off and the dog runs by.
Most knowledge is pretending.
Expressing it, metonymy.

11.

The wind got up on the library terrace and dark cloud
fell over red St Pancras. Where will this blow us now
there's so much to complete and the world has finished?

12.

Obscurity and anonymity—these were the coordinates.
The wind came across and the sky grew dark.
People were killing for some verses they believed in.

13.

Development of epic. Sea water; loyalties; netherworld
hallucinations. And a cheerful resolution where the
shambles of the voyage echoes, germinating recapitulation.

14.

Falcon chased off by a couple of crows whose
chutzpah was engendered in a DNA that Pleistocene
hunters encrypted in their jokes and stories.

15.

An old black poplar where Little
Owls have nested. Decades of east
London tattooed into their elocution.

16.

These secondary presences, spirit
siblings, half unborn simulacra, don't
exist, then they do, as nouns stagger

down the pencil from some
unvoiced suspension: and yet nothing
from those old back staples is depleted,

and these vehicles are harmless, carry
nothing and are nothing, have no origin,
no body, travel nowhere, denote nothing

but some ritualised join or re-configuration.
Breath, too, works elsewhere: most especially
never on this sterile one-dimensioned

plain with its flotsam of parched,
black hieroglyphic flora.
Phonological time passes unvoiced over metal.

17.

Ratiocination hence! Avaunt encapsulation,
reference, involution and this
busy-bodying of the hyper-expressive.

Dry Mud Scratches

1.

The page had worn thin so I biked
out to the marsh and walked against
the wind towards this solitary kestrel.

2.

Insignia I may not read.
What the bird sees it wants and needs.
Then feeds in deep grasses.

3.

Hoofs impressed dactylically in mud
mark lines whose pauses lie alongside
clues of long, serrated bicycle elastic.

4.

In dry trodden circles and
small broken grass stems
an uneventful narrative emerges.

5.

Who spoke the Ur-word on which
everyone has written commentaries?
The *akara* and *aleph* contain all phenomena.

6.

A small, red-tiled signal box inscribed with
white graffiti stands ruined among pylons
that threaten to engulf it in their live cat's cradle.

7.

In asymmetric shreds:
'*mes sentiments . . . à Londres . . . tendres . . .*'
in the strangling bindweed and seeding thistles.

8.

(One fragment on a plantain leaf intelligibly
planted: '*c'est toujours*' at the edge.
And a thumb print in the autumn sunlight.)

9.

Never mind the hard bike ride home.
The poplars are performing their equinoctial fugue.
Each leaf striking the wind's persuasion.

10.

Late. A stone crossing. Causeway
unmarked and the water encroaching.
Warte nur. A little darkness falling. *Sei geduldig.*

Everywhere Wrong Bodies

1.

I am that other, along with all the others
in this crush, impersonally shoving.
We are everyone wrong bodies.

2.

Sehnsucht: yearning and displacement.
Ah, how lacking.
But what good fortune for a minor poet!

3.

Working out a costume. The character
of thought that breaks over a face,
infringing the initial undefined creation.

4.

Famous to us for his obscurity. And in
his bursting mind a prince of the cosmos
who exchanged stations with angels.

5.

Grass seed sprouts in the wall crack dust.
Just ahead of the cart she continues to trundle,
a shadowy abbreviated vista opens.

6.

This ravenous, emaciated saurian on the
rampage through your upholstery: you have
failed to tame it with your kind good humour.

For as much as it feeds on that hospitable diet,
its hunger is sharpened, and your softness whets
the scythe-edge of its indigestible and bitter harvest.

7.

As the flowers for which we longed transcend
their perfection and crumble into rubbish,
it's the compost that begins to matter.

8.

Bad light. River weeds. A girl's back, panicked
by a mountain wind that's passed through bay
trees, from whose stink she runs crying.

9.

The *twa corbies* it was that pecked at the
gentleman. Thus he became *anatkuq*: stumbling
on his bones and unconscionably tweeting.

10.

Old men who walk uneasily on
working days with knowledge of
so much that's become inexpressible.

11.

The hooded panting of dogs. Ludic
floundering of adolescence. Old man
in headphones. Two decades of nothing.

12.

He worked to follow nature
and the garden embraced him.
United at last with the compost he'd started.

High Tea in Victoria

1.

High tea in Victoria. Golden rod pollen
in bomb-site rubble. Crusted with black market
dragées, thinly iced cake and room-temperature trifle.

2.

Scoured chalk fields in autumn.
Blue flint. Dead weeds, fence
posts. Uninterpolated silence.

3.

No answer from the void to my
outcast rootless cry. Flap up in lark
song, little Tudor varlet!

4.

Buzzards calmly float in the ring of these
bashed-up old binocular lenses, scarcely
distinguishable from the accumulated debris.

5.

Up against the hawthorn, sheep are
rubbing their peaceful faces, determined
that I join them in the pastoral continuity.

6.

Martins mill suddenly across the ridges
exposing their chests at a hundred angles.
Soon they'll be flashing across Spain and Africa.

7.

In the valley, motor cycles overtaking one
another. Up here, some red admirals, and
somewhere on my thumb a small black spider.

8.

Glider in white-and-blue Peter
Lanyon downs-sky. Dragonflies
hawking and one distant bird call.

9.

A turfy old mound and a circle
of hawthorns sacred to the wind
that hourly twists them.

10.

A small moth torn off by a sudden gust
of air. At the end of the wood, a panel
of unevenly fragmented windows.

Sehnsucht Nectar

1.

From dreams and disease
a triumph of
submission to the imperfect.

2.

(Located thus however in
the flaw, lay all we wanted
of an *ich/du* separation.)

3.

Small bird, when I cried *Thou*, I was still
far from close as you chirruped through
the blossom where no *We* compounds us.

4.

If there hadn't been a paradox, there might
have been no marriage. And without
that divergence, no poetry either.

5.

You requested an exemption. But
however few selves you claim beneath
your jacket, the patchwork's still showing.

6.

Listen to the sea—the blank verse
of its current. I thought we'd lost
touch. But the moon's still rhyming.

7.

Lacrimae rerum. What things
cry out
for us to express them?

8.

Sarve dharmah dukkhitah.
Our constituent moments accumulate
within the evolutionary disaster.

9.

That I'm still here contemplating my discomfort
is a kind of paradise with internal, domestic serpent:
a hermaphrodite that lays plentifully.

10.

Thank you, sacred individual: for your husband.
Without him I'd've been ill with hope.
And this, indefinably, might have been fatal.

11.

The grumbling of hymenoptera,
and a harrowing fission
that split this jar of sunlight

from its genius in the forest.
Sehnsucht zieht uns an
through firefly vapour

that turns blossom to mango.
O thorns-and-honey
kāvya: as of bees in anger,

you have swarmed on the
connectives. Hard to renounce
that fructifying conjunction.

IV

No Pavilion in the Mountains

1.

If by some chance I found myself just
once in this thirteenth century landscape
and could empty the mind of its interruptions . . .

But the scroll-ends have rushed back
and knocked against each other,
and thus stimulated by exclusion,
I must stand at the margin

and eavesdrop on the uninterpretable crepitation
of its textual characters, while the
rivers and mountains, geologically reversed,
sink underneath the black swarm overwhelming them.

2.

After spring rain, the clouds have fallen into the pines,
the graduated layers of whose branches are half-weighted
down in this confusion of earth and lower heaven,

and there's nothing now to separate us anywhere from
the ten thousand things that have been engendered.

3.

Is it more than we should hope that the waterfall that rushes off-
centre towards this surprisingly intact little bridge in the valley
will have ceased to vibrate with the chemistry of ink on paper?

It makes such coarse roaring. But a passage it must have,
and the rocks and trees can only drink and then give way
in recognition that resistance would intensify the pressure.

4.

Tall sparse bamboo sprouts, with their
ideal separation, giving us the air in which
to speculate between their stems and foliage,

have struggled among rocks to achieve this
condition and someone, soon in the autumn,
will prune them away so next spring will
generate the same spectacle of balance.

5.

What are these pines sketched in for, so close
to us, along the paper? A dim horizon,
like the bleak stuff of hardship,
confirms both a texture and a point of vantage.

6.

A superannuated carp hangs
in the temple pool and its rimmed lips
gape in counter-rhythm to its gills and belly.

Its balloon-rubber mouthpiece
gasps up, slack now, boiled rice,
fish scraps, kitchen rubbish.

After the October snow has settled,
some old monk will cook it gently.

7.

The poet has gained the top face of the plateau.
Behind him, forests, gorges and the half-hidden
roof of a contemplative pavilion. He gazes down
at the drop and above into the void. There's nothing
further to accomplish. He might step into the chasm.

8.

It's both senseless and helpful to go on
longing for these empty mountains.

Striated from the brush, they exacerbate
and slake this thirst for dissolution.

The claims on their pages
are abstruse. Their aridity fecund.

9.

So much would drop away by this tree
I found that stood without thought
no distance from the place I had imagined.

What grew generated no identity but rose
flexibly with the season. The wind conditioned
its shifts of angle. That slight visual difference.

10.

He might be a scholar (the difference isn't
great) or it could be a peasant, bearing this
double-chambered gourd along space

between the rock and water and where
little exists beyond a rushing upward
of the mountain and the movement of a

river in which change never changes.
And the trees? They're dragons which
the rock and water have made grow

from one another. A tree also becomes rock.
And rock, within itself, conducts itself

through water. There never was a scholar.
Nor could it have really been a peasant.

Starting as a Ruin

1.

I'd prefer to use stone.
For birds and plants
to weather. Starting as a ruin.

2.

Between the dead hollyhocks and kitchen
window, a labyrinth cross-hatched
with this violin partita. Spiders' shambles.

3.

Rough old meadow.
Sedge trashed by summer.
A few thistles aborting.

4.

Hornet squatting by an excavation in this small
scabby apple, grasps in front of it a large wet
half-fermented crumb and knowledgeably munches.

5.

Thin autumn varnish and the sedges are
rehearsing their September death cry.
They've stuck out their season.

6.

While the afternoon is finishing,
that small gate stands against the
foliage. It grows darker to go through it.

7.

A compulsion to this fall of night.
Steadily it moves to every object.
That fire in a cloud, optimistic and deluded.

8.

Translating bare branches—blue still
with damsons and alive with finches—
to this season will be problematic.

9.

A scum build up at the hidden
sluice gate. Pressed into itself, the
water takes on a cast of the metal.

10.

At last I can see the blue face of the
tractor that up beyond the Mill House
willows had sincerely laboured.

11.

Throb of some old clock. A smell
of dust and its erotic hush. Time
presses on our breathing.

12.

Bell-fade and the clock tocks onward.
Cold light on the flushwork. Past
and future. Same wind on the ruins.

13.

Face against the landscape. Little
hilltop dwellings. The path of an ascetic.
A narrow quattrocento quiet.

14.

Orchard and wheat field.
Sour cherry strudel.
A baked inland harvest.

The Sibyl at Avernus

1.

Before I was subordinated to this career
of indecorous excitement,
I had a small herd of goats and lived
in unremarkable obscurity
without all the fuss implied by spiritual intoxication.

The soul is not a subsistence product
that can be dried or salted down.
It feeds on air, light, movement, sensuality, friendship.

But he has plucked me out and stuck me
in this end-stopped corridor of grottoes.
There I indite his brilliant, twisted animations.

I've been left with nothing:
a nine hundred year old girl
whom the god has deranged
and who trades on his dictation.
I've become an old pickle.

2.

What started as a hiccup progressed to an
electrifying retching, on the crest of which
quavered a portentous conundrum.

Now I am corrupted, his dialect's
become my patter: a rhetoric of less
sense than these chestnut-leaf scratches.

3.

Once subordinated to the music
of his hoo-ha, it was easy to divine what
songs he wanted. Having wound
me up to a hexameter, the god separated
from the vortex and constructed me
this grotto in which I could unravel.
Scarified by asphodel and now that
he's inside me, the god's made me his virgin.
I'm burned black by his shadow.

4.

Night after day, eviscerated as a cinder
in this single-person city,
I choke up his mottos

which through friable,
degenerating niches
express this or that message.

5.

The webbed patter of dactyls. Imponderable spondees.
Dry through the cave mouth, hexameters of stone and foliage
picked up at Cumae in contaminated flashes.
Virgil strolled here so they tell me.

6.

The great emptiness is everywhere.
Beyond the sea and its limestone horizon,
more and merely more of nothing.
All this is all I have. It's this eludes me.

7.

A window in the rock across which
young elm branches wave and—
as the wind deals them—tenuously settle.
Everything else is unaccountable.

Blown about at the threshold, my jumbled inditements
in this heap of dry leaves proclaim
some or other human future.

I will never see Rome. But carry in my brain
the long, slow collapse of amphitheatre masonry.

8.

An absolute truth is the nonsense to which
you encouraged me, and my interlocutors have
become habituated to my agitation. This, you reassure me,
is what they expect of an art or religion.

Since it's all I can perform, I resign myself to their enchantment.
The river god's daughter had a preferable destiny.
She who is evergreen, peaceful, quick-stemmed, unconscious.

Virgil at Cumae — Circling Avernus

1.

Those young men jumping ashore at Cumae
did finally grab the flints whose ignition,
from a distance, generated so much trouble.

2.

The Sibyl: a melancholy old witch
who had integrated that one brush
with Apollo with her psychological musings.

3.

What did you mean 'underworld'?
Everything on the surface
is, by definition, infernal.

4.

The masonry of your hexameters
built of stone which had been
conditioned already by pre-history.

5.

Grumbling into a nekuia. Crusts of tufa
come off on the sandal, revealing spirits
pursuing infernal careers within the magma.

6.

You who sail between the islands, black cup lifted,
took mild steps towards each beckoning edge to
fill it with the blood that took on your reflection.

7.

No, it was not dark. She led me down
as if I were a canary with my
endogenously optimistic soprano lighting.

8.

On the shores of Avernus I sat down
to eat lunch: sheep's cheese and an
apple whose core I chucked
down to this stinging nettle *katabasis*.

9.

Shades through the culvert have been
left to spiral downward. By
three cinder blocks proleptically abraded.

10.

From Gasthaus Hell he'd jogged vehemently up
and was careful not to slip on windfalls rolled
out from an orchard to Avernus' water.

11.

The dog I saw. Its silhouette against
a long, low wall. It was fetching
for the dead and smiled with the effort.

Note to the Reader

All the pieces in each sequence are separate poems except where indicated by punctuation.

Notes

Most of the pieces in this volume have been inspired by translations from Japanese and Chinese poetry that I have been reading since the late 1950s. I have not tried to write in any precise form. But beautiful elements of internal contradiction found in many of Basho's *hokku* certainly represent an influence.

No Pond Moment

Introduction

In a memoir of his time with the poet Matsuo Basho (1643/44 to 1694), Shiko, one of Basho's students, wrote:

> The poem was written by our master on a spring day. He was sitting in his riverside house in Edo, bending his ears to the soft cooing of a pigeon in the quiet rain. There was a mild wind in the air, and one or two petals of cherry blossom were falling gently to the ground. It was the kind of day you often have in late March—so perfect that you want it to last for ever. Now and then in the garden was heard the sound of frogs jumping into the water. Our master was deeply immersed in meditation, but finally he came out with the second half of the poem,

> A frog jumped into water—
> A deep resonance.

> One of the students [the poet Kikaku] sitting with him immediately suggested for the first half of the poem,

> Amidst the flowers
> Of the yellow rose.

> Our master thought for a while, but finally decided on

Breaking the silence
Of an ancient pond.

The student's suggestion is admittedly picturesque and beautiful but our master's choice, being simpler, contains more truth in it. It is only he who has dug deep into the mystery of the universe that can choose a phrase like this.
(Matsuo Basho: *The Narrow Road to the Deep North and Other Travel Sketches*, translated and introduced by Noboyuki Yuasa, Penguin Books, 1966:32)

Because of our familiarity of Basho's haiku, it is easy to lose sight of the strangeness and originality of both the poem and the context of its composition. For many (I include myself here), Basho has attained, on account of both his poetry and his journeys through Japan, a quasi-mythological status. He has become for us a Buddha of early modernism whose frequent expressions of suffering do nothing to diminish our esteem for his Buddhist insight and poetic genius. In the context of this and our own contemplation of his frog poem, it is natural to imagine the poet alone by the pond, while the silence is broken by the frog entering the water. Shiko's narrative disabuses us of this expectation. Not only is Basho set apart from the pond but he is in company (presumably on the veranda of his little house whose garden abuts the river). Nor is the noise of any one frog alone in breaking the (comparative) silence. There are poets on the veranda and the air outside is alive with wind, rain, bird song and frogs jumping and croaking. (Croaking frogs, *naku kawazu,* are a commonplace of earlier Japanese poetry. Basho's translation of sound from a frog to the water is one his *hokku's* innovations.)

Our conventional response to the poem may not, however, be entirely wrong. After all, most readers will not have enjoyed access to Shiko's memoir. It must therefore be reasonable to imagine the master alone in a garden where all that happens is what he describes. A moment such as this of Buddhist insight is impossible to convey: but it shares the nature of a Zen face slap or the breaking open of a Rinzai Zen *koan.* Set against this, Shiko's narrative interestingly suggests a combination of sociality and reclusion. Where the circumstances of an enlightenment experience is concerned no either / or is required. How and where such an event occurs has no relevance.

Compounding this absence of any quasi-absolutist reclusion, we learn that the poem emerged not only in two fragments that had been separated by another poet's intervention, but that it was also completed in conversation. Of course the exchange between Basho and (the celebrated) Kikaku represented a version of linked verse (*renga*) practice. In this, poets composed mutually allusive pieces in response to the stimulus of a 'head verse' (*hokku*) which had been given by a senior practitioner. Indeed in 1686, the year Basho composed his poem, saw the publication of an anthology called *Kawazu Awase* ('Frog Contest') consisting of frog poems by several authors suggested by the *hokku* that Basho had made famous.

Still, the circumstantial details scarcely compromise what otherwise the poem suggests. Quite separate from or within the environment in which the poem emerged, resides a contemplative space in which nothing else does happen. However many other frogs, birds, cherry blossoms, rain drops and wind gusts there might have been at that moment, a frog still jumped, broke the water, interrupted the silence and returned it to what it had been. The timelessness of this 'circumstance' lives easily within the social conditionality of the poetic event. Likewise the *hokku*'s 'spiritual' import dwells within the commonplace. As Japanese monks seldom tired of repeating, there is nothing special in Zen. And as Basho insisted:

> What is important is to keep our mind high in the world of true understanding, and returning to the world of our daily experience to seek therein the truth of beauty. No matter what we may be doing at a given moment, we must not forget it has a bearing upon our everlasting self which is poetry (Yuasa 1966:28).

Notes to poems

4. These are Matsuo Basho's dates. The word *basho* means 'plantain tree' and the poet adopted this name after somebody donated a plantain to the patch of ground outside the poet's hut. The tree was planted in 1680 and some years later Basho wrote: 'I love the tree for its very uselessness ... I sit underneath it and enjoy the wind and rain that blow against it.' Because its trunk contains no hardwood, the plantain is a Buddhist symbol for impermanence.

5. The leptodactylid is a species of frog.

6. The blue laces belong to sandals that were donated to Basho in the course of his journey described in *The Narrow Road to the Deep North*.

7. The Indian monk Bodhidharma who travelled to China in the early 6th century was the first Ch'an [Zen] patriarch. He is said to have meditated in a cave somewhere in southern China for nine years before agreeing to engage in teaching. Japanese tradition depicts him with ferociously staring eye balls.

10. Basho's term for frog is *kawazu*. Another word is *kaeru*, whose alternative meanings are *to change* and *to go home*.

15. Two aspects of lotus lore crop up in this series. In Hindu tradition, the universe is conceived as a lotus growing from the navel of the god Vishnu as he dreams the cosmos into being from the pre-creational waters. In Hindu-Buddhist iconography, the lotus also represents a final stage of spiritual evolution (for which 'purity' is a frequently used shorthand). One Sanksrit term for lotus is *pankaja*: 'mud-born'. The word (pungently) encapsulates the fact that the lotus is rooted in mud and its long stem works its way to the surface on which perfect and unmuddied blossoms open.

19. The etymology of 'extol' is from Latin *ferro, ferre, tuli, latum* 'to lift' (such was one pillar of a mid-20th century private education). The verb is used largely for its assonantal function. 'Ten thousand' is a Buddhist/ Daoist symbol for multiplicity.

39. The head is filled with crazy and unrealised thoughts, feelings and impulses. Courtiers, editors and diplomats, however, educate themselves to transmute these psychic materials into conversation: a rare talent which sometimes also finds expression in creative sublimation. Poetry in particular is a means of making emends for solecism and verbal misbehaviour. And it is the alchemy, albeit in the idiom of *esprit d'escalier*, which applies gold to the scar that weighs down consciousness with a sense of its own baseness. Montaigne compares the compression and perhaps sublimation that occurs in poetry with musical sound production: 'just as the voice of the trumpet rings out clearer and

stronger for being forced through a narrow tube, so a saying leaps forth much more vigorously when compressed into the rhythms of poetry, striking me then with a livelier shock.' (*On Educating Children*, trans. M.A. Screech). Stendhal and Chekhov were great students of inappropriate speechifying and amends-making. In effect we all live within the same comic opera with its variably disastrous consequences and dénouement. Walter Raleigh knew this:

> Thus march we playing to our latest rest.
> Only we die in earnest. That's no jest.

40. Avalokiteshvara is the *bodhisattva* (enlightenment being) of compassion in Mahayana Buddhism. The reference here is to the *bodhisattva*'s place in the *Heart Sutra* in which he/she looks down through the cosmos and proclaims the doctrine that all *dharmas* or phenomena are empty of character. The *Heart Sutra*, along with the *Lankavatara* and the *Diamond Cutter* Sutras are relatively late texts whose Sanskrit versions were taken to China in the 6th century, and which became the foundation of Chinese Ch'an. This was introduced to Japan in the 10th century and became Zen.

The final line derives from a story of one of the Buddha's previous lives in which a monkey deceives a crocodile which has been lusting to eat his monkey wife's heart. See *The Jataka—Stories of the Buddha's Former Births,* ed. E.B. Cowell, 1895 Book 2, no.208. The line is also indebted to a book by Peter Khoroche titled *Once the Buddha was a Monkey*, a translation of Arya Sura's *Jatakamala*.

In the context of Japanese literary tradition, the idea behind the verse as a whole derives from a new poetic formulation instituted by Basho and his followers, who amalgamated secular and sacred, vulgar and refined, popular and aristocratic idioms in their poetry.

44. This poem, the first stanza in particular, most likely represent a self-parody.

hiragana — Japanese cursive or running script.

51. *dukkha* — Sanskrit and Pali: suffering.

52. This piece might be paraphrased as follows:

That individuality is compound, and that both frog and poet consist of squamous or scaled, layers of identity and that this is carried throughout the accumulations of personal history. Even a frog, identical as it appears to individuals of another species, hops its own path, volitionally or not. And humans, albeit quintessentially all the same, of course at least appear more different from each other than frogs seem from the point of view of the human. Marks of human individuality are adaptive. We seem to want them and they are an element of our success as members of a species.

But in Zen contemplation 'custom' or conventional, socially adaptive self-definition, may be abandoned; and one may become a bit more like what one imagines a frog to be. In other words, a relatively undifferentiated and anonymous component of the natural world. One may, nonetheless, in the very process of detachment from custom, or in taking the plunge towards assimilation into the characterless water of the pond, paradoxically, acquire an identity at just that moment of self-departure. This is precisely when the self's reflection registers and the poet reinforces this with acknowledgement of the moment. The tension of our skin and water tension meet and the artefact of the poem ('here on') is one product of this and survives whatever may have occurred within the historical moment (frogs do, after all, exist, and the poem emerged as the frog really jumped in). And there's reason to assume that many people—and this may have been Basho's experience—did undergo the process of depersonalisation while also being conscious of it in some way, whether or not this registration was simultaneous or post hoc, theoretical, intuitive, momentary or suggested as a desideratum. I'm not, of course, attempting to speak for Basho. But rather attempting a generalisation about some aspects of the experience of his poem.

This note was written in an email response to a phone message left by Roger Langley in which he requested an explanation to the phrase 'squamous individuality'. In fact the entire sequence was initiated a day or so after I had shown Roger the poem by Sengai which projects Basho into the pond with the frog. I would like to take this opportunity to dedicate the whole sequence to Roger Langley with respect, and in friendship.

53. 'Basho jumped'. The initial phrase is quoted from the poet painter Sengai (1750–1837). And that other comedian Ryokan (1758–1831) wrote: 'A new pond/Not even the sound of/a frog jumping in.'

54. *usuk* — Inupiaq (north Alaskan Eskimo) for the *membrum virile.* Trickster in native American myth was represented variously as quasi-human, coyote, raven, hare. Hunger-driven fool or semi-divine demiurge he [sic] underwent the misfortunes and humiliations of the idiots found in many folk traditions.

Conversation with Murasaki

This sequence suggested itself some years ago while I was still reading *The Tale of Genji,* and the attempt to write in response to a literature which I could only dimly comprehend was complicated by feelings of cultural trespass, aesthetic impertinence and a sense, not least, of historical anachronism. In the latter connection, I had chosen the form of the short, free-standing poem known since the late nineteenth century as *haiku,* though the models I knew belonged mostly to Basho's *haikai* genre in which seventeen syllable *hokku* verses either formed introductory pieces in multiply authored series or were embedded in prose works such as Basho's own travel writings. Second, the often subversively vernacular and contrary *haikai/hokku* idiom which Basho transformed did not exist in Murasaki's time. Indeed, the action of the *Genji* probably took place during an idealised early generation of Kyoto's Heian period (9th–10th centuries) and much of its narrative is constructed around the exchange of classical verses (*waka*), many of which themselves allude to poetries of an even deeper past. The discord between this world and that of a twenty-first century writer with no knowledge of Japanese remains a source of embarrassment, but this very discomfort also became part of the incentive to impose myself on the fugitive but tantalisingly amiable persona of Murasaki Shikibu. As repeatedly suggested in Murasaki's writing, social and erotic relations were conducted within the most stringent proprieties whose rules the main characters spend much of their lives breaking or reformulating in their own interest. My poems are therefore, in one sense, versions of these (male) escapades. There is also a philosophical anachronism.

The characters in the *Genji* belong to a world in which salvationist Pure Land Buddhism coexisted with Buddhistically modified shaman traditions, both of which were alien to the Zen which arrived two centuries later and informed aspects of the *haikai* idiom developed in the seventeenth century by Basho and his contemporaries. Zen, I think, might not have been dreamy enough for Murasaki. And perhaps this would have been something she could have agreed about with her court rival Sei Shonagon who surely would have relegated Zen to one of her 'Disagreeable Things' lists.

1. Murasaki Shikibu: born ca. 973; author of *The Tale of Genji*. The name Murasaki means 'purple'. The first two syllables of her other (inherited and official) name mean 'wisteria'. See also poem 5.

2. Sei Shonagon: contemporary of Murasaki and author of *The Pillow Book*.

19. *sutras*: Buddhist texts

21. *anicca*: Pali, impermanence

29. There is still, I think, a For Sale notice outside Arthur Waley's house. In visibly accumulated dust and scatterings of stationary, traces of his DNA remain in tension with the 'no self' doctrine suggested in this poem. Waley's *Genji* translation (1921–33) remains, in itself, a major work of literature. Later versions by Seidensticker and Tyler perhaps make for clearer reading.

30. *Mono no aware*: 'the pitiful transience of existence'.

32. Ambitabha: the Buddha of the Western Paradise or Pure Land.

Hototogisu

The *hototogisu* is the Japanese cuckoo, Cuculus poliocephalus, which has figured in Japanese literature at least since the eighth century. Unlike the European cuckoo with its two-note major/minor interval call, this species has a musical, if hurried and anxious, five-note warble. According to folk tradition, the *hototogisu* emerges from the underworld at rice-planting time in spring and its call is associated with painful memory and love sorrow. Murasaki's *Genji*, Chapter 52 contains this passage:

> The fourth month came . . . The scent of the orange blossoms near the veranda brought memories. A cuckoo called and called a second time as it flew overhead. 'Should you stop by her dwelling, O cuckoo.' His heart heavy with memory and yearning, he broke off a spring of orange blossom and sent it with a poem to Nijo . . .

> 'Its sings in the field its muted song of the dead.
> You muted sobs may have joined it to no avail.'

The singing cuckoo was also believed to cough blood, and it was partly this thought and the bird's passage between the upper and lower worlds that gave the *hototogisu* its exquisite but fateful identity.

Generally through the sequence, the words cuckoo and *hototogisu* are used with variable Japanese or European association and there are places when they are confused or counterpointed jokingly.

14. 'Spondee and anapaest': this alludes to the *hototogisu*'s song metre which corresponds roughly to those same prosodic feet: - - u u - . (the song can be heard at http://nwbc.jp/singing/)

The same poem also alludes to the rhythm of the term hototogisu itself. As pronounced by a Japanese speaker, the word carries no particular stress. An English voice, however, will naturally stress syllable 1, thereby lending it a metrical value approximating the final line of a verse in Sapphic metre (- UU - -). Line 3 quotes *lumina nocte* ([bright] eyes at night) from one of Catullus's sapphics (Cat. Carm. LI). The Latin phrase doesn't make sense out of context, though light and darkness associated with the *hototogisu* is suggested.

Incidentally, Catullus, too, imagined an underworld journey for a small bird, Lesbia's dead sparrow, in Cat. Carm. III:

> Qui nunc it per iter tenebricosum
> Illuc unde negant redire quemquem.

'Now he takes the dark road from which, people say, nobody returns.'

20. *ava-tili-guvvaq*: Inupiaq (north Alaskan Eskimo) for 'snow bunting', a tiny bird that migrates north in spring and harbingers the whale's arrival. It features in a widely-distributed fable in which it mourns a dead husband.

Existence Mazurkas

son filé — 'spun out tone': a long legato line bowed on a stringed instrument

Dragonfly Intelligence

1. This is the habit of *Anax imperator* (the Emperor dragonfly).

2. Where the dragonfly was remains part of its habitat and it, or some fellow specimen, will return to the roost position which is identified (albeit invisibly) by its having been there.

3. This is the species *Calyopterix splendens*, which like all dragonfly species, practices an aerobatic sexual yoga.

4. The female dragonfly oviposits by pushing the tip of her abdomen into water or aquatic weeds and debris.

6. This describes one of the genus *Sympetrium* which commonly basks on warm surfaces, often at ground level. See also no. 15

7. One of several large dragonflies of the *Aeshna* genus, many of which are hard to distinguish from each other at long range.

8. *Enalagma cyathagerum* is one of two common sky-blue and black patterned damselflies. One extra thoracic stripe separates it from *Coenagrion puella*.

9. This is Linnaeus as I imagined him then. But many other European divines of the past three hundred years have contributed to natural history observation and the classification of plants and animals.

10. The dragonfly larva or nymph is acquatic and frequently accelerates by squirting water from a valve at the tip of its abdomen. Two males of the *Libellulid* (middle sized) species have a plum-skin-bloom-like powder blue abdominal colour.

12. The first and third words are in the imperative.

14. *Libellula quadrimaculata* is a strongly flying pan-European migrant. Its body is dark-beer-coloured and, as its name suggests, it is marked by spots at the base of each wing.

15. Fossils of about seven hundred species of dragonfly from as early as the Carboniferous era have been recorded. See also no. 6 for the 'darter' species alluded to here.

19. The *Zygoptera* are damselflies: a sub order of the order Odanata (toothed insects). I was compelled, somewhat pedantically, to speak to higher authority on this matter.

The Poverty of Pots and Jars

By poverty I wanted to suggest bare existence, in that the pot or the jar stands merely as and for itself, and whether it has aesthetic or utilitarian purpose, it proclaims nothing beyond its own contour. Of course elegance and utility often coincide and ritual function may also attach. Every pot has emerged from the earth and in its passage through the hands has transcended earth while retaining part of its original character. This is one surviving expression of a connection we maintain with the ancient people who first achieved these marvellous interactions between nature, aesthetics, domesticity and ritual.

Co-existing with those mysteries lies the relationship between the interior of the pot and its exterior form: for the concave inside is fashioned by and in relationship with the convexity of its surface. But while its outside is embraced by the light and has its place among objects and people, the interior remains largely invisible: it co-exists with the world that the outer pot inhabits but it is also a preserve of separation and obscurity—indeed, it *is* those values. This dark inside is, nonetheless, part of, sometimes largely, the pot's *raison d'être,* for it is there to be filled. But while its high-baked walls are built to preserve liquids or to keep cereals or sacred relics dry, intact or protected from the uninitiated, the pot, in its quintessential character, is defined by emptiness. Whether it contains wine, oil, wheat, jam, bones, texts or nothing at all (in the case of ornamental ceramics, the interior is a modest converse to the decorative virtuoso display area), it remains simply a container and its inner space, whether crammed full or empty, is a not-self which is a condition or a reflex of the positive materiality of its outer form. And yet this non-identity is essential: all pots have it. Whether this shared element, whatever the pot's shape, is common to all the countless pots that there have been, is impossible to say. All these factors intersect with or belong to one another, just as pots belong to the earth from which they have been forced to take leave, and all of them are surrounded by the same air that inhabits the interior until the latter is filled and the space inside 'becomes' or is displaced by something else. The *Heart Sutra* of Mahayana Buddhism proclaims 'Form is emptiness and emptiness is form.' The Japanese tea ceremony with its emphasis on the ambiguous nature of earthy, spiritualised, functional, beautiful and often asymmetrically only-half-pleasing utensils provides one context in which to contemplate that teaching. I am grateful to Daniela Zimmermann, who is writing about the phenomenology of pots and jars, for enlivening my very amateur acquaintance with these thoughts and issues.

Pre-dynastic Essays

These poems were written in the Petrie Museum (University College, London) which contains the largest collection of pre-dynastic terra cottas outside Egypt.

Notebook Hokku

The shorter forms in the book were suggested and inspired by Japanese and Chinese poetry, but I have not attempted to write *haiku*. The title of this sequence is nearest I've come to admitting that some of the poems, in this section particularly, represent haiku echoes. For more on *hokku* see note to *Conversation with Murasaki*.

Secondary Presences

Secondary presences are the poems in this and other sequences. It is hard to determine how much of a writer's persona inhabits any poetry and how far this latter maintains a life of its own which mixes artefacture with the conscious and unconscious impulses that generate it. Perhaps more important here was to observe the phenomenon of writing as a cultural habit. No doubt it is a common experience for artists to perceive themselves as members of a craft or guild: and rather as one imagines an Egyptian scribe carving hieroglyphs or a cathedral mason on a scaffold, so watching the pencil as it follows the hand or is dragged across the page, represents an aptly depersonalising process of self-reflection.

14. The animal fables I learned and sometimes saw enacted in Alaska are more or less universal. There were fragmentary little stories associated with the most obscure Arctic cliff tops and beaches whose more or less precise elements I later discovered in Sanskrit and other unconnected literatures such as Grimms' *Märchen*. The Inupiaq (north west Alaskan Eskimo) epics that I recorded in the 1970s appear to be confabulations of these same short, percussive animal narratives. Or possibility the reverse: the epic came first and dispersed into fragments. It is easy when you observe inter- or intra-species encounters in the flesh (almost invariably they're about quarrelling, mating, feeding) to see how these tales came to be. And it is possible that all literatures, including the European epics (alluded to in no. 13), represent a derivation of this ancient genre. The behaviour of the birds I saw on Walthamstow marshes was also typical of the activity of the same or similar species in the Native American stories.

15. These owls and poplars co-exist with the birds of no. 14. It is said that a number of animal species do have regional accents, though I'm not sure if these correspond to identifiable human phonologies.

16. Poetry writing, like most activity, presumably represents some kind of ritual behaviour, but this has been partly obscured by the print medium and even by handwriting.

Dry Mud Scratches

5. *akara* and *aleph* : the Sanskrit and Hebrew vowels *a*.

15. *Warte nur . . . Sei geduldig: only wait / you too will be at peace*
The first phrase is from Goethe's *Wanderers Nachtlied II:*

> Über allen Gipfeln
> Ist Ruh,
> In allen Wipfeln
> Spürest du
> Kaum einen Hauch;
> Die Vögelein schweigen im Walde,
> Warte nur, balde
> Ruhest du auch!

The second phrase, 'be patient' (not in Goethe) is a self-admonition.

The stone crossing—to some nameless underworld—was evoked by a passage in the final movement of Schubert's piano sonata no. 20 in A.

Everywhere Wrong Bodies

9. The human drama of the *Twa Corbies* ballad is framed by a beast fable, while the talking corbies (ravens) also suggest that the dead knight has suffered a tragic but dreamlike quasi-shamanistic (*anatkuq*) initiation.

High Tea in Victoria

dragées—a round and slightly larger variety of 'hundreds and thousands' used in cake decoration

Sehnsucht Nectar

Sehnsucht: yearning.
Sarve dharmah dukkhitah: Buddhist Sanskrit: 'all phenomena are characterised by suffering.'
kāvya — classical Sanskrit poetry; here obliquely alluding to the *Gitagovinda* of Jayadeva.
Sehnsucht zieht uns an: longing draws us on. A corruption of Goethe's Das Ewig Weibliche zieht uns hinan: 'the eternal feminine draws us onward.' *Faust* Part 2.

No Pavilion in the Mountains

I wrote these poems when I was studying some 12th and 13th century Chinese brush paintings. With the exception of the scene depicted in no.10, the landscapes are imaginary and no specific scrolls or scenes are described. The circumstances are imagined to be those of Taoist/ Buddhist contemplatives who retired from public life to live in mountainous southern retreats following the fall of north China to the Mongol Khanate in the thirteenth century. A number of these so-called literati poets and painters may have lived out their days in this sort of idealised seclusion and thereby established a semi-legendary hermetic tradition.

www.ingramcontent.com/pod-product-compliance
Lightning Source LLC
Chambersburg PA
CBHW022156080426
42734CB00006B/461